ARSONIST

ANHINGA PRESS

ARSONIST

JOAQUÍN ZIHUATANEJO

2017 ANHINGA-ROBERT DANA PRIZE

Selected by Eduardo C. Corral

ANHINGA PRESS

TALLAHASSEE, FLORIDA 2018

Copyright © Joaquín Zihuatanejo 2018
All rights reserved under
International and Pan-American Copyright Conventions.

No portion of this book may be reproduced in any form without the written permission of
the publisher, except by a reviewer, who may quote brief passages in connection with a review
for a magazine or newspaper.

Cover Image: Joaquín Zihuatanejo
Design, production: Jay Snodgrass
Type Styles: body text in Minion and titles in Aktiv Grotesk

Library of Congress Cataloging-in-Publication Data
Arsonist — First Edition
ISBN — 978-1-934695-59-3
Library of Congress Cataloging Card Number — 2018939217

Anhinga Press Inc. is a nonprofit corporation dedicated wholly to the
publication and appreciation of fine poetry and other literary genres.

For personal orders, catalogs, and information, write to:

ANHINGA PRESS
P.O. Box 3665 • Tallahassee, Florida 32315
Website: www.anhingapress.org • Email: info@anhingapress.org

Published in the United States by Anhinga Press
Tallahassee, Florida • First Edition, 2018

THE ANHINGA-ROBERT DANA PRIZE WINNERS

2017 Joaquín Zihuatanejo Arsonist

2016 Hauntie To Whitey & the Cracker Jack

2015 Elizabeth A.I. Powell Willy Loman's Reckless Daughter
or Living Truthfully Under Imaginary Circumstances

2014 Robin Beth Schaer Shipbreaking

2013 Bethany Schultz Hurst Miss Lost Nation

2012 Anna Ross If a Storm

2011 Rosalynde Vas Dias Only Blue Body

2010 Kimberly Burwick Horses in the Cathedral

2009 Gretchen Steele Pratt One Island

2008 Rhett Iseman Trull The Real Warnings

2007 Kenneth Hart Uh Oh Time

2006 Meredith Walters All you have to do is ask

2005 Sandy Longhorn Blood Almanac

2004 Joshua Poteat Ornithologies

2003 Deborah Landau Orchidelirium

2002 Erika Meitner Inventory at the All-night Drugstore

2001 Patti White Tackle Box

2000 Ruth L. Schwartz Singular Bodies

1999 Kathleen Wakefield Notations on the Visible World

1998 Julia B. Levine Practicing for Heaven

1997 Michele Wolf Conversations During Sleep

1996 Keith Ratzlaff Man Under a Pear Tree

1995 Ann Neelon Easter Vigil

1994 Frank X. Gaspar Mass for the Grace of a Happy Death

1993 Janet Holmes The Physicist at the Mall

1992 Earl S. Braggs Hat Dancer Blue

1991 Jean Monahan Hands

1989 Nick Bozanic The Long Drive Home

1988 Julianne Seeman Enough Light to See

1987 Will Wells Conversing with the Light

1986 Robert Levy The Whistle Maker

1985 Judith Kitchen Perennials

1984 Sherry Rind The Hawk in the Backyard

1983 Ricardo Pau-Llosa Sorting Metaphors

for our fathers who were there

our fathers who were not

and our fathers who were both

You don't know me, not really. And I hate to tell you like this, but my father—
I mean, our father, has died.

—from a Facebook message I received while writing these poems

CONTENTS

I. CAUSES OF DEGRADATION

CAUSES OF DEGRADATION (A SEQUENCE)

II. ARSONIST

III. OCCUPY WHITENESS

ARSONIST

I. CAUSES OF DEGRADATION

father buried in the earth beneath grass,

beneath flowers I trample as I run.

—Kim Addonizio

YOU CANNOT ESCAPE BLOOD

Alone. On the hike. You blame him for your carelessness. August. There is ample water but the temperature is well over 100 degrees. You have crossed the creek six times. Less than a mile from the falls you lose your footing. Skeletal arms go out too gaunt for wings. Though it was only several feet you land with a dull thud on a large rounded boulder. Pain. But this is different. It is so close to the center of you.

There where the seventh rib meets the sternum. Breath leaves you. Your eyes tear up instantly. After seconds of silence there is air. You gasp. Then scream. Alone. You crawl into the stream. Let cold mountain water cascade over you falling onto your chest. Numb. You pull yourself onto the bottomland. Lay on river rocks. The high noon sun directly above reminds you that nothing forgives. Eyes closed.

You notice your lip is bleeding. The taste of warm copper in your mouth. A thought enters your mind. *You cannot escape blood.* You try so hard. But cannot remember who said this to you. You remember it in English, not Spanish. So it cannot be the men who raised you. Maybe a professor. Perhaps your father whispering it to you in a dream. You roll over. Place one arm under the other. Push up slowly. Stand.

Bent at the waist. More question mark than man. You turn. Wince. Look to all sides of you. It is true. You are alone. You place one foot in front of the other. Slowly. Ache. It hits you. Something deep inside of you is broken. It is too soon to know if it is bone, flesh, or something else. It doesn't take long to realize it only hurts when you step in a downward motion. And every step from this point on is down.

GIVE HER ONLY ONE WORD

Papermate pens, pocket knives, watch bands, money clips, a deck of cards (the suicide king is missing). A death has brought you both to this. The home. Is not yours. You are not a guest. She is older than you. Likely in late forties. She. Blonde and petite. You cannot tell if her eyes are green, blue, or some unnamable color. You recall your tío telling you years ago, never trust a person with eyes a color you cannot name. She is what this country calls beautiful. For a moment you consider her beautiful. A motionless pendulum hangs in the New Haven. Dust outlines on floral wallpaper where photos of father once hung. She approaches you. Calls you a name that is not yours. Smiles as she directs you to cashier. Informs the woman behind the adding machine that your name is Juan. Tells the woman who is less blonde, less petite than she, that from time to time you mow their front and back yard. She instructs the woman to sell you the books for 50 cents each instead of a dollar. The hardback copy of Four Quartets by Eliot is a First Edition American version. You know this. She does not. You know that despite its condition it is worth a few hundred dollars. She smiles at you. Puts her hand on your shoulder. It's all too familiar. You want to shout in her face. Do not touch me. But you don't. She calls you a name that is not yours again. You recall your tío telling you at a young age they will always see you as Mexican first. American second. She. Thanks you for all you have done to make her home beautiful. You. Smile at her. Give her only one word. *Gracias.* You gladly pay three dollars for a stack of rare and vintage books.

In this way you dance
on her father's grave. You dance
on your father's grave.

NOVA

Snow. The day you are born. Such unusual weather for the desert you inherit. But you refuse to let this story begin with white. So you change it. Rain. The day you are born. Such unusual weather for the desert you inherit. Your father. Stands outside the emergency room doors. A soft pack of Camel Straights in his hand. His swimming pool eyes a stark contrast to the grey sky above. No. There will be no white transitions in this story. His sunless eyes a stark contrast to traceries of azure above. Your mother screams. Pushes you into the world after 17 hours of labor. The nose and mouth are suctioned. You take your first breath. Cry. Your father. Silent as benzene. Exhales white smoke through both nostrils. Stop. You will not allow intangible whiteness to appear in this story. Your father. Silent as arsenic. Exhales smoke more blue than wan through both nostrils. She. Places the baby against her flesh. You refuse to latch. Exhausted. Your mother rests from the pain of birth. Closes her eyes. He. Places the key in ignition. It cranks. But refuses to start. Flooded. Your father leans back on the headrest. Closes his eyes. On the radio Stewart begs Maggie to wake. With a furious rattle and hum the big block V8 turns over. You cannot recall if the Chevy is pearl or silver. This is all a story whispered to you. By an uncle who rises crudo and angry on Sunday mornings. Call the car black. Call the father back. Blue blanket. Brown skin. No getting around those hospital walls. Anemic. Bloodless. Impossibly white.

THE BREADTH OF OUR DISCONNECTION

or

ON FINDING OUT THAT I WAS LEFT OUT OF MY FATHER'S OBITUARY

He is survived by sheets soiled crimson. Crumpled cold on hospital floor. Survived by blood in lungs, throat, and mouth. Hair in sink. By chemotherapy, by diagnosis. Survived by pain in side and shortness of breath. By calloused hands, farm jack, come-along, whirligig. He is survived by new family and new priorities. By community college art classes. By not so brown boy. By (the idea of) beautiful brown woman. He is survived by pills of different colors and sizes. By PTSD, by Agent Orange. He is survived by severed limbs and wails of soldiers too young for death. By Ho Chi Minh City. Unit, Corp, God, and Country. Act I of Hamlet. By Paint by Numbers. Survived by amniotic fluid in lungs, throat, and mouth. By unbuckled belt and floral print dress on the floorboard of a Chevy. By young man and younger woman swaying in time in small town Texas dance hall. He is survived by "I'm So Lonesome I Could Cry" playing on the jukebox.

PYRITE

My father is flesh rotting. My father is thermal rising. My father is hawks circling west of Baby Head Cemetery near Llano County. My father died. Holding his hand out for me. To stop. He did not want me near him. My father died. In the line of this poem. In the lie of this poem. I did not want him to hear me. I stand near the bargain bin. Outside the bookstore. The only one I know that's purple. *The Reckoning* in my hand. The smell of Camel cigarettes. An open palm across my face. I close my eyes. Search for an image of my father's hands. Search for words to make something new from all that is old. Search the white marble quarry looking for quartz, jasper, and gold. We find only pyrite. A boy. A fool. And all that glitters.

IRIS

The attendance sheet read Ricardo,
but if you say your name is Iris, then it is.
Don't answer to anything else.

—from a student's yearbook I signed years ago.

Iris at war with flesh—blossom rising from ribbed dirt earth—sheer panties silk blouse—captured in polaroids when house is bare—hidden from father—in sock drawer with diary and mother's merlot lipstick—Iris curses stubble contour of muscle and bone—desperate for efflorescence—let imaginal cells transubstantiate— she pats her heart three times—believes in holometabolism—just a fancy word for correcting God's carelessness—soft as iris petals—hard as Blackland clay—Iris does not answer to man—fag—bitch—please don't make her bring you to knees— she can't help the fact you hate what you covet—Iris fears hollow moon—empty men—heavy voices—slurred by bottom shelf—smell of piss behind the It'll Do Club—Iris is skin tight black and silver sequin dress—Jeffrey Campbell boots— ironclad Joan—nude Andromeda—

Marionette girl
armed with dull scissors—she wants
to be and not to be

FOR THE PRIVILEGE
OF KICKING YOU ONCE

*After "Every Hard Rapper's Father Ever: Father Of The Year" by Douglas Kearney
and the Argument Between My Abuelo and My Father at My Naming Ceremony*

because it rhymes with walking
stalking brown women
all that idle Faulkner talk
she, wet seed wild
he, hot blind sun
we must be

because it rhymes with mocking
new world ball-hawking
shucking our gods—I mean crops
locking your doors
keep on knockin'
but you can't

because it rhymes with fucking
a tousled Puebla dress
a cowboy belt unbuckling
an infant's lips suckling
a father's fist knuckling
it all evaporates when you lean on it

THE CORNER OF BONITA BLVD & HENDERSON AVE

The mother acknowledges the baby without smiling. The baby acknowledges the black and white television through mesh lining. Inside the magic box Graciela Mauri sobs. Trapped in her Toy World.

The throb of wooden spoon on floral print enamel stockpot. The mother stirs guiso on the stove, the smell of ajo, serrano, comino. The baby stirs in the playpen now strong enough to roll over.

Steel springs under the mattress murmur. Shell of woman weeps silently into his pillow. The baby's shrill cries reverberate through the sparsely furnished room filling their hollow world with sound.

The mother lifts her slender arm in the darkness toward the muted door. The baby lifts his fleshy arm in the darkness toward the mute blonde light peeking out from under the door.

BONES

5 & 4
(Center Field)

In the center of the
field a rust colored Dodge
towers above goose grass
its bumper bent upward
a crooked smile on a
blushing face of metal.

4 & 4
(Like Mom and Dad)

Now, I must tell you both,
that just because you
turned your backs on me
does not mean I cannot
see you staring back
at me by the river's edge.

6 & 6
(Midnight)

Yerba Buena blooms for us
at midnight under the
foolish moon, you said
in a brackish voice deep
as well water waxing
through notion and age.

5 & 5
(Pair of Sunflowers)

Some things grow best in
muck and mire. They grew
in the alley adjacent to
nothing where fists flailed
flesh. Ceremony can
easily save or slay.

4 & 4
(The Windows)

The windows overlooked
the garden where cebolla
jalapeños and herbs
grew, where a child knelt
in brown earth & thanked
the life giving soil.

1 & 1
(Snake Eyes)

It's not enough to cut
off the snake's head, we
bury it. Our eyes full
of what the elders called
la tristesa de la
vida. Hands, dirt, venom.

REMAIN(S)

then the news comes to you from a stranger.
connected to you by your father's blood.
by the idea of blood.
of what remains.

and let our fathers remain motionless.
until acted upon by force.
silent as bottomland.
unforgiving as sun.

and let us breathe in our fathers' remains.
let our fathers remain within us.
remain without us.
remain.

CONFABULATION

You're all fiction writers.
> —Lidia Yuknavitch

So desperate are you to fill in the _____ with what was once there. Your _____ left you and your _____ before the _____ of memory. He returned once to give you a _____ which you used to bring _____ into view. What did you learn from looking up at all that _____?

A. Celestial bodies like our _____ are beautiful but _____.
B. Nearness is so important to a _____ child.
C. You _____ your father. You _____ your father. You _____ your father.
D. _____ of the above

XOYACALTITLAN

A home or a place of decay

What you hear
Dried cochineal beetles
Crushed in molcajete
What you feel
Florid warmth rivers
Onto maguey fiber
Much too common for cotton

A framed seascape shatters against hard wood floors

What you hear
Canon fire
What you feel
A rapier
Slicing through tongue
Leaving you
Silent as shorn flesh

The slamming of a door

HOUSE FIRES

The house stands erect
today, but my family
burned down long ago.

The mother scattered
as ashes do, caught beneath
boot soles of strange men.

Camel cigarette
smoke. Rancid Brut aftershave.
His smell. Lingers. Still.

Children born of cin-
der and story labor but
fail to quell the flames.

STARVE

She sculpts mold away from the edge of the loaf

no ajo in the sopa seething on the stove

in the center of you

cord of bone-dry Toro is wrenched

but you feel hunger in fingertips before the gut

from the pull-out couch in the sala

you can see the doorknob

                                        ineffable face with austere backing

such delicately carved brass

                                        outside the pane the fixed blink cycle begins

red   red   red

                                        all you ever wanted was your father

to starve

CAUSES OF DEGRADATION

(A SEQUENCE)

I. AIR POLLUTION

She left the photos up for a while
you hung over us like sulfur
dioxide visible and invisible
                                    my
smile on your face in the
polaroids
        I took them down one
night as she slept
                hid them from
her in a boy's desperate attempt to
clear the air
                a son will do anything
to help his mother   breathe easier

II. FIRES

So many nights she pulled the lit unfiltered Camel
from between your lips
she told me more than once
you almost burned us to the ground as we slept
when you leave something unattended
negligently discard cigarettes, sons, and all such small things

you turn flesh into debris

the ultimate goal of the arsonist is to destroy wholly or in part

III. OVEREXPLOITATION

You tried so hard to ruin us

with your carelessness

hands covered in paint

above a once blank canvass,

an over-abstraction

just a fancy word for prolonged periods of drought

IV. LOGGING

you   uprooted   sapling
piñon   nogalito   chisos
stripped it & left it bare
there was no way to hold
the soil   in place

V. INSECTS

surely you must know
encroachment of any kind
can contribute to the loss

    of

            something

                                small

                and

                           rare

VI. PESTS AND VEGETATION DISEASES

Eventually I poured gasoline on the photos
set them ablaze

cleansing by fire

I watched our faces blacken in the flame

any poison meant to kill the predator
will eventually destroy the prey

VII. FIREWOOD SCAVENGING

In the darkest part of the forest moss grows so deep that walking makes no sound
This is how you slipped away into the ink shoes in one hand flint in the other
Silently searching for cattails fungus compressed flower tops to catch the spark
When you apply heat but starve it of breath the ember becomes highly combustible

VIII. ANIMAL FORAGING

If given the choice
we would rather freeze
                than starve
Even in winter
we would seek farther
forage longer than our fathers
we came to know intense shivering
and slurred speech in an intimate way

IX. PASTURING AND OVERGRAZING

It is uncertain how long the recovery period will last we should have known
something wild and non-native would refuse to take root in such an arid place

X. INDUSTRIALIZATION

there
was
nothing
natural

about
the
rhythm
we creatd

there
was
never
a homeland

to be lost

XI. URBANIZATION

Fatherless   boys
find   each   other
become   brothers
bound   to   one another
by   the   want   of   blood
though   shifting   variables
make   predictions
about   future   growth
next   to   impossible
some   things   were   certain
natural   causes   included
earthquakes,   storms,
and   wild   boys
setting   photos   on   fire
economic   impact
was a child support check
that   bounced
over-   population
was   three   brothers
sleeping on a fold out couch
in   the   living   room
extinction was a cop car
parked   on   the   corner
of   Bonita   Boulevard
and   Mañana   Avenue
it   was   all   so close
so   far away

II. ARSONIST

I want to give you something, or I want to take
something from you. But I want to feel the exchange.

—Ada Limón

ARCHETYPES

3

I will tell you three things about my father and one will be a lie: my father left the year I was born; my father's heart like mine and yours is made up of four chambers, but only three work well; my father's left atrium broke the day he walked away from me.

There were three of us. We all came from different fathers, but the same mother. We all have different colored eyes but the same smile.

We're all different but the same. We're all different but the same. We're all different but the same.

4

I think I have only loved four women well in my life.

At some point you should take all the money in your wallet and spend it on the women in your life that you have loved well. At the moment, counting the change in my pocket I currently have just under seven dollars on me. I would buy the first woman a white peach because she once moaned after biting into one. I would buy the second one a pack of sugar free gum because she is diabetic. I would buy the third one a disposable camera, which seems insignificant, but oh, can you imagine the possibilities in those 24 exposures? The fourth woman, I would give this poem, as I would likely be out of money at this point. This section of this poem says as much about the fourth woman's love of poetry as it does about my ability to budget money well.

I'm writing this poem in an airport. My flight lands at 4:00 PM, and there's a very good chance my phone will be dead by then. When I land, I don't want to call the four women I've loved well, I want to call all the women I did not love well and tell them just how sorry I am.

I'm sorry. I'm sorry. I'm sorry. I'm sorry.

7

My favorite movie growing up as a kid was The Magnificent Seven. A remake of a classic Japanese film, The Seven Samurai. In terms of film, my favorite childhood movie is an American bastard, but it's a good one. So am I. So are my brothers. You could teach a class on archetypal symbolism from just that film alone.

The star of that film, Yule Brenner, died of lung cancer. Just before he died he shot one of the most powerful and poignant public service announcements. That PSA ends with Yule Brenner staring into your soul from inside the black and white television repeating three words, just... don't...smoke. I swear it must have run seven times a night during the prime time of my youth. And though I can't be certain of it, I think those may have been Yule Brenner's last words.

When I was seven I learned that my father smoked unfiltered Camels, so did Yule Brenner. And though I can't be certain of it, I think in the end it will not be my father's metaphorical broken heart nor will it be his actual broken heart that gets the best of him, in the end it will be his lungs. And I, his first-born son, will not be there to hold his hand when he dies. I will not hear his last words. I will not ask for or accept his forgiveness. In the end there will only be silence.

I forgive you. I forgive you. I forgive you. I forgive you. I forgive you. I forgive you. I forgive you.

I just found out my flight is delayed. It will not land until 7:00 PM. Will the women I have not loved well forgive me for my silence, or for the times I should have been silent but was not? Will they forgive my carelessness with money, or my carelessness with all four chambers of the human heart? Will they forgive me for loving words more than I loved them? Will they forgive me for all the poems I've written about them or all the poems I haven't written about them?

I want to write a collection of 28 poems. Seven poems for each of the four women I have loved well. And though I love them all, I will reserve the use of closed form for only one of them. I will write her seven Shakespearean sonnets. No, I will write her seven villanelles. No, I will write her seven epic poems written in rhyming couplets. No, I will write her seven powerful and poignant PSA's that will all end the same, with three words, repeating.

I love you. I love you. I love you. I love you. I love you. I love you. I love you.

ANOTHER KIND OF FAITH

Somehow they heard about us. We, an inner city team from the lower east side that had not been beaten. They, a premier league team from some far-off foreign suburb that could not be beaten. The game was inevitable. It was Manifest Destiny. The Great Western Movement. The Alamo. The Mexican American War.

Were they any more American than us? Their team name, The Cowboys. Ours, Aztecas. You cannot write this. Sometimes it simply is.

It is simple. Good guys wear white, bad guys wear black. We moved as murmurations during warm ups. They nervously sized us up. Days earlier, they invited us to their facility. That's what they called it, a "facility." In the barrio we played on a field that was two-thirds dirt, one-third dream.

The night before the game I dreamed of war. We were armed with staffs, spears, bows and arrows. They with muskets and swords. I watched my friend die beside me.

A "friendly," that's the word they used, but there wasn't anything friendly about it.

Jesús Santos, my best friend. Jesús Santos, our best player. Jesús Santos, I watched you die in my dream. How many days before you rise and save us from our rage.

Some of us played with rage in our hearts, but not Jesús. Only someone pure of heart could bend a ball like him. He was our savior. And we his ten disciples.

Ten minutes into the game Jesús scored the first goal. They answered not long after, on a two on one breakaway.

They wanted to break us because we were different. We wanted to break them because they were beautiful.

Jesús was a thing of beauty. Watching him weave through defenders his eye never on the ball always ahead; it was part of him. He slept with a soccer ball, kicked one to school and back home again. Left it outside the church on Sunday morning resting on the steps waiting for him. A small practice goal in his back yard. A different position. A different placement. A different scenario in his mind each time. 100 shots on goal every day of his youth.

100 shots X 365 days = another kind of faith.

This was another kind of cruelty. This was brutal. Five on one. Cowboys vs Indian. This was less slide and more tackle. The wounded knee of the most beautiful soccer player to have ever lived. This was freight train made of legs and arms, fists and cleats. Jesús Santos laid out on the field arms outstretched wailing in agony. Crucifixion.

They had turned us into beasts. Made us more Mexican and less American that day.

The fight that ensued was viscous. Boys were not meant to fight like that, but sometimes war cannot be avoided. Sometimes war is there waiting for you all along.

It is a simple thing to hate the way we did that day.

Days earlier I had dreamt of war, watched my friend die beside me. Jesús Santos are you still out there? Did your heart break that day? Jesús please tell me, does one have to be either different or beautiful? Is it possible that one can be both?

NAHUI OCELOTL

Special was not the word we used for Corky in the barrio. I'll ask you to understand we wore our callousness the way we wore our dirty T-shirts and torn jeans, because it was all we had back then.

We would not call Corky retarded in front of his father. Corky's father was as large as he was quiet. He was not large and quiet the way a live oak is large and quiet. He was large and quiet the way a volcano is large and quiet.

We were hunters that day. Manny Valdez and I. Armed with the weapon his mother had given him months earlier for Christmas. Why would anyone give a skinny brown kid with a curse word for the world such a thing?

She purchased the Crossman Model 766 for Manny at a garage sale. A pneumatic BB repeater .177 caliber pellet single shot. It was the first variant with tapered plastic bubbled housing instead of wood.

The loading mechanism however was broken, to load it we had to point the barrel to the sky, drop a pellet in and make sure our angle of shot was straight and never downward. We were at war with gravity.

Our friend Jose said to us, "I like this pellet gun, how we have to load it. It makes me feel like we're settlers loading a musket." Manny replied, "No way Jose, we're Indians who stole it from settlers. Now we use it against them."

We were laying on Manny's porch hidden behind shrubs armed to shoot white joggers that ran up Bonita Blvd through our barrio on their way to Glencoe Park and the wealthy white neighborhood that lay just beyond.

The pellets would strike them like angry metallic wasps. They'd slap the back of their necks, jerk frantically. Startled into a full on sprint as they cursed the air. We'd duck and laugh our asses off.

Though the sun was high and bright, thunder could be heard in the distance. It was Manny, the musket, and I. He drew a bead on one of Corky's five dogs. "Pinche perros always shitting in my yard."

Corky's father worked on an old lawn mower in his front yard while their dogs defecated all over Corky's yard, Manny's yard, and just about every front yard on that particular block of Bonita Boulevard.

Then we noticed the Jaguar. Something so beautiful had no business being on Bonita Boulevard. The automatic window rolled down and a man with an accent thick as mesquite bush leaned his bulk out the window.

"Amigo...amigo...you need a job? 'Cause I could use a good yardman."

"Cut your own grass you pinche cracker."

Corky's father always had a way with words.

"You go back to Mexico, you no good wetback! You hear me wetback, you go the hell back to where you came from! And keep your god damn dogs out the street, or I swear to God I'll run those sons of bitches over!"

Then the Jaguar sped off up Bonita Boulevard in the direction of Glencoe Park. But not before we fired three shots at the black beast. We had never loaded and pumped the rifle so fast. Three shots. One hit.

A partial victory. But we took no joy in it. As we noticed Corky's father tousle his son's hair and smile, we knew we were nothing more than two fatherless warriors armed with the idea of a musket at war with the idea of our fathers.

NAHUI EHECATL

SECOND SON WIND SUN

"I am different things on different days."
—My tío Silastino

Under piñon swaying with wind. Thinking of the brother my mother gave away the year I turned six. What is it to lose something—before you knew it was yours to lose? I have not seen my brother in a lifetime. I don't drink. Never had the stomach for it. My eyes close. I am sitting on a porch with my brother. The same breeze on both our faces. Drinking ice-cold Budweisers, laughing, cursing like our tíos did when we were mocosos. He has a daughter now. Like our mother she sees through inkwells. Hair as long and ebon as a cormorant's wing. Our mother. Was always his—he was only hers for a short while. Just long enough to teach us one thing:

the greatest act of love any mother can do for her first son
is to give up her second son
to save them both.

My eyes open

and I am son and nothing more.

NAHUI QUIAHUITL

THIRD SON RAIN SUN

> *"Down on the bottom, down to the last drop in the cup.*
> *Down on the bottom, no place to go but up."*
> —Bob Dylan and Jim James

In my dream my brother carried me across the river. With each step he took I grew heavier. Pockets full of coins I stole from the offertory basket. I touched the cross that dangled from my neck. Tlaloc grew angry. Rain came. The river swelled.

On one side
my tíos dance
their arms flail toward us
crowned in feather headed-dresses
chachayotes around both legs
the sound of dulcet rain on tin shed roof
they sing
>> *In can on nemian noyollo yehua?*
>> *In can on nemian noyollo yehua?*
>> *In can on nemian noyollo yehua?*

On the other side
my Abuelo kneels
crowned not with thorns
but sharp prongs of the cotton plant
the blood dripped onto the hassock
beneath his sore knees
a voice deep as well water questions
>> *Crees en Dios,*
>> *Padre todopoderoso,*
>> *creador del cielo y de la tierra?*

My fingers dig into the bottomland. Reaching back, he was gone. Cristóbal, Cristóbal, Cristóbal. Say his name three times. Pat my heart three times. Dance. Sing. Pray. This is what the dream said to me. Do not be this. Or that. Be both. Let God be in the church and in the rain. Let crowns be made of feathers and thorns. Let the man on the cross grow hummingbird wings. Let the river wash me away. Let my brother rise. A golden carp. Let me be lost. Let him be found.

FOR YOUR DAMN LOVE

Your mother was a devout Catholic. Your father was an atheist. You are intentionally using the past tense. She is now Mormon. He is now dead. For this reason and so many others you constantly find yourself praying to nothing. You search for the sacred in the night sky, an empty hand, a plastic bag with a large hole in it. Since his death, everything has a hole in it. Including you. How is that you mourn so deeply, weep in an empty hotel room late at night over a man who left all those years ago and never came back? They gave you an explanation. An obituary. So many words. Sentences. Paragraphs. There is no mention of you in the body. You are a something reduced to a nothing. A dried riverbed. A forgotten secret. A roll of exposed film. You recall the photograph of him that you burned as a child. His foolish, resplendent body so thin and skeletal. The right angles of his shoulders. The terse edges of his elbows. It is because of him that every part of you is sharp. Knuckles. Knees. Tongue. You inherited that much from him. You do not tell your mother that your father is dead. You do not see the point. She has been remarried for many years. She only ever talked about your father in her sleep. You wake late at night from the ache of hunger. Sit up. Let your legs dangle over the fold out couch. The only bed you knew as a child. You walk past her bedroom door on the way to the kitchen. You learn from her that it is possible for someone to cry in their sleep. You can only make out one word between sobs. His name. Which is also yours. Many months after hearing the news you call your mother. Ask her how she is doing. Make small talk. Say it in passing.

My father is dead.

She is silent.

She is a new moon. A callous palm. A torn grocery bag dancing within wind in a vacant parking lot. She severs the silence with pointed gossip about a distant cousin. Scolds the dog in Spanish for knocking over the water bowl. Such piercing indifference. You can hear her story on the television behind her. She will not carry this with you. You are using the present tense intentionally. Half of your past is gone forever. The other half refuses to acknowledge that any of it happened/ happens. And there you are. A boy standing in front of a grey metal trash can in the alley that parallels Bonita Boulevard. A photo of a slender, blonde man in one hand. Your tío's Zippo lighter in the other. Above you a hollow moon lingers. In the distance a gurgling borracho sings Por Tu Maldito Amor. Beautifully. You close your eyes. Hear a voice that might be the drunk man's, or your father's, or yours. Whisper. Burn it. Turn it all to ash. And warm yourself by the embers.

MESTIZO

I watch as they take the Host. Swallow Him. Let Him dissolve into nothingness. Break Him. Bite Him. The priest's hands so close to gum and spit, tongue and teeth. They line up to receive Him. Bow their heads. Acknowledge their unworthiness to accept such a gift. Crudo. Beaten. Broken. Made whole by want, they step aside, drink from the chalice. Some drink longer than others, longer than they should. Father frowns when they do. I see Father mix water with wine, long before mass begins. He says it is part of the miracle. Jose says it has more to do with money. He is older, has served the church longer. He tells me there is only so much money for wine, only so much miracle to go around.

Transubstantiation.
Pat my heart three times,
Believe in miracles.

Finally, I bite the flesh. Drink the blood. One half altar boy, one half vampire. Dark marrow, pale face. Mestizo balls to bones. This. That. Neither. Father tousles my hair. Takes what little wine we have left back to be poured in with the rest. He does not know from time to time, we steal sips when he is not looking. I know it is sin, but choose to call it something else.

PRESA NO MÁS

para mis hijas

No van a escuchar tu voz. Sólo verán su rostro moreno, así que si yo cazo el cazador lo hago para protegerte. He visto a cubrir sus pistas cuando se realiza la massacre, pero sé que una manada de lobos cuando huelo un solo. Así que corremos. Como un conjunto. Corremos. A ser escuchado.

Toman el pueblo.
No dejan el fuego. Quemamos
nuestros antepasados en la pira.

Deje que las llamas crecen más y más alto. Para que puedan ver que todavía estamos aquí. Y hemos crecido con hambre. Así que voy a enseñar a mi joven para no cazar por el bien de la venganza. *La venganza es mejor dejar en los manos de Dios.* Ellas simplemente cazar por el bien de su hambre.

Harán fuego
Del cuchillo y piedra. Ellas se chupan
la médula del hueso.

Algunas lecciones nacen de la hambruna y el fuego. Las pieles que se apilarán. La carne se dore. Entonces ellas sabrán lo que he aprendido, la carne del lobo sabe como miedo.

PREY NO MORE

for my daughters

They will not hear your voice. They will only see your brown face, so if I hunt the hunter I do it to
protect you. I have seen them cover their tracks when the slaughter is done, but I know a pack
of wolves when I smell one. So we run. As a herd. We run. To be heard.

They take the village.
Leave us the fire. We burn
our ancestors in the pyre.

Let the flames grow higher and higher. So they can see we are still here. And we've grown
hungry. So I will teach my young to hunt not for the sake of revenge. *Revenge is best left in the
hands of God.* They will hunt simply for the sake of their hunger.

They will make fire
from knife and stone. They will suck
marrow from the bone.

Some lessons are born of famine and fire. The pelts they will stack. The meat they will sear.
Then they will know what I have learned, the flesh of the wolf tastes just like fear.

FOOL MOON PANTOUM

She carried worlds within her womb. He was crowned by a towheaded sun. Constantly eclipsed by an irrational moon. I was his son. Born to a sandy-haired man I did not know. Contstantly eclipsed by shadow. Just another kind of celestial body.

The washed-out man I did not know was dutiful, distant, and cold. Always out of arms' reach. Like every other kind of celestial body. Beautiful, resistant, and bold—I wanted to be everything he was not. Never out of arms' reach. To the ones who needed me most.

I wanted to be everything she was not. More than blind sky and oblivious star. To the ones who needed me most. Be more father and less ghost. She was the witching hour sky. He was the gravepassing flash. She more flesh. He more ghost. I was a child with arms raised in the dark.

It's funny. A careless sun always settles for a foolish moon. It's true. Some children are raised in the dark, but they grow despite the darkness.

VISITING HOURS

1

Tortillas blacken on comal,

The smell of cornfields ablaze,
charred husks blister then rise like murmurations.

Hinges groan as bed folds back into couch;

Our people gave the world the concept of zero.

Key turning ignites engine;
a boy's hand becomes diving bird outside truck window
in the cab a corrido is sung;

strangled sobbing;

candles on altar in sala glow;
pine forest bisected by asphalt;

carcass rots in the sun;

overhead, shell made of black feathers;

key turning opens cell;
when do visiting hours begin?

2

I lay on the hood of a 1984 Chevrolet Monte Carlo,
a plastic bag dances within wind,
you shatter the reflection of constellations
with stone a boy's need for destruction.

Tonight the smell of rain lingers;
tomorrow morning, we will wake sore
in the neck from seats that will not lean back;
you whisper to me in the darkness,
something about la llorona and death,
Is that the best you got, I ask?
Somewhere in the black
a frog or toad hops into the water.
You join me on the hood as I gaze at night sky,
silent, so I ask again, Is that the best you got?

They're all dead you know, the stars we gaze at.

ON A BED THAT WAS NOT OURS

We said so many things that could have ended all this. We both wanted it to end. Afraid of something as weighty as contour of flesh entangled on a bed that was not ours. Light through curtains on your knees, my hands. Cotton sheets separated us from the rest of the world. No idea what time it was only that there was light and

nothing else between us.

We lay there lost and found in our own awkward nakedness. You whispered something unspeakable to me about you…your father. Something you had never said aloud. "Unforgivable," the word you used. Before you finished I interrupted with, "I forgive you." But was clumsy and wrong to say so. What I should have said was

there is nothing to forgive.

CEREMENT

a child's palms, a window sill
worn rough from years of neglect

on the other side of the pane, his tío
holds a body more marionette than woman

sangre
mas sangre

the storm
a knife on the floor

her limbs and neck
slight and wilting

eyes
open and vacuous

her cerement
a night gown more red than white

his muted reflection
the same but different

a boy in the rain
a shade of pink found only in severed flesh

in the darkness
outside the window where it all happened/happens

on a boulevard
whose name translates to *pretty* from Spanish

REQUISITE FOR A FLESHY EMBRACE

she gave me the tempest,

the deftness to find poetry in things most find vile,

the open palms, poems, truth,

but above all a requisite for a fleshy embrace.

he gave me the temper,

the daftness to love art more than flesh,

the closed fists, stories, lies,

but above all a weakness for the sound of applause.

when the time comes

bury half of me in sacred ground.

the other half leave in the woods.

let the scavengers devour me piece by piece.

THE LENGTHS

The chain link fence divorced two worlds
  the dying St. Augustine under corpulent live oak
   the alley that paralleled Bonita Boulevard

where turbid rainwater puddled in potholes
  the taste of sweat on our lips, oppressive air too thick to breathe

the alley alive with hundreds, maybe thousands of mosquitoes.
  I watched Jesús walk into the scourge
   shirtless, eyes closed, arms outstretched.

The unwonted lengths one will go to
  to feel anything but the life they are given.

AWAKENING

after Rainer Maria Rilke

With box elder and Mexican flame
lush as bosque beneath gray anvil
sheets of cinereous upland cotton
veil a bed that was once ours.

And down from your neck
the flesh of your arms, to your wrists,
a word written on each palm.
Left hand, stay. Right hand, awake.

Crown fashioned from huisache thorns,
the silence cuts into you.
You will still be able to sleep
without me beside you.

ARSONIST

after she extinguished the flames
the son was nothing more than ash

to lay with her
men walked through the boy shaped pile

of cinder on the splintered floor
look and you will find him

between soot and ink
an initial incident

the turning of a doorknob
the striking of a match

flesh and blood a poor substitute
for dazzle and despair

GÜERO

you boy formed from sand

                on Bonita Boulevard
                in barrio eastside

your familia
calls you güero.

                your best friend
                boy forged from bronze

almond shaped eyes,
he does not realize

                that you love him
                and envy him

at the same time.

SUNDOWNING

for J, who no longer recognizes his wife and daughters

Though dusk

falls too soon,

I will not think

of it as black,

but rather blue.

The glimpse of light

in the hue

will be you.

FOR BETTER OR WORSE

Almost a year now

what I've learned is this:

> my dead father

> is not in the dirt,

> nor is he in the poems—

> he is in me.

III. OCCUPY WHITENESS

It responds to insult and attempted erasure simply by asserting presence

—Claudia Rankine

SESTINA FRONTERA

de la misma manera

we more akin to dark than light

cursed for Spanish tongues

for whom death gapes

with bruised hands and heels

we stay low give watchmen the slip

we, just another kind of silt

eso es lo que la gente quiere que le esplique

climb from river wash away silt

move quickly travel lightly

cuidado, silently sideslip

wrap sharp American syllables around tongues

beware the coyote, the heel

you run, pant, your mouth gapes

es verdad

this new country, this language gap

nothing more than dreams and silt

trained dogs fresh on heels

run to darkness, run from light

slow your breath, silence tongue

let water slip through lips

y le dirémas

las mujeres in dresses lower their slips

arid canyon walls gape

silence chattering teeth with tongues

use hands to carve a bed in silt

pray to the Virgin's horned moon for light

don't wish for home, don't click your heels

creo que de seos solo hay uno: yo

when morning comes walk softly, toe then heel

through the bosque you quietly slip

question your prayers do not trust the light

la migra hungry to close the gap

smooth out your skirt dust off the silt

tilt heads to ground stifle tongues

si se deciden a hablar

let the rolled r fall from your tongues

pick up the pace, push with your heels

you, more than river, more than silt

more than mistake, more than slip

familia awaits, their arms agape

run, claw, fight for the light

aquí está, todo suyo

speak lightly, hold tongue

a gaping wound called faith, here you are healed

baptized by river slip and earthly silt

ROOTED IN THE VERGE

for Isidro

There where grapes

and brown boys grow.

                                             I opened my eyes

            vineyards

            how they grow up from ground

            and overhead.

                                         I recall how impossible this seemed.

Hearing God

                                       on still air

whisper in your ear,

You were born to be caged.

            Do you feel free

            when you taste your wine?

No need to read it in books

migrant boys can tell you

all you need to know of slavery

       rows of shack homes

       shared by multiple families

       hard dirt packed floors

       communal bathroom

       toilet stalls without doors

       because brown boys can't afford

       the privilege of privacy

       even while shitting.

                  Clouds came full over, and thunder

the morning storm did not linger,

                  it drifted by indifferently.

There where sons rise

but do not shine.

       There where brown boys give

sweat and blood

to the soil.

They were growing

hooked onto vines

rooted in the verge.

Can you tell

where their hands end

and earth begins?

THE ROW BETWEEN US

Can   poem   be

                                     bandera
drenched   in   surrender?

Pull   white   pickup   off   road
and   into   the   turn   row.

                                   We   come   to
dirt   in   a   close   way.

Take   the   penknife   out,   jab
at   one   of   the   rows.

                                   What   lies   rooted

                  in   voice.

                                   They
                                   cotton

effortless

secrets in earth

ashes, everything sacred

lifts up in flat clod.

We

digging a little deeper uncover

the loam,
do not spare the harrow

wrestle with white,

ache return find
field
spreads
before us.

Untiring.

Fingers bleed

under

water jug.

                    So   much   blood,

so   little   water
to   replenish   this   dry
landscape.

          We   return.   Reap.

One   of   the   cotton   seeds
          sprouted   bent   double   broken.

In   October   another
grandchild born
where   only   white   grows,
only   brown

                        thoughts

we   might   not
make   it.

We   emerge   into   blinding   noon.
Son   will   not   forgive   father.

A   little   further   up   the
row   finds   the   same   thing,

angered

                                        reminders   of
our   chasm,

man

                        and   God

so   careless.   White.   Brown.

The   row   between   us.

WINTER, 1984

Wind   caught against

                 the flesh—a boy,
                 a coin in hand

                 December came brought with it the ink
                 Qué tristeza the needle brings

      Gurgling borrachos sang to hum of engines—idling red lights on Henderson

                 three blocks down to the mercado

      The power night possessed made monstrosities of raw craven men
      who took their wives to construction sites late at night so the city
      would muffle their screams as their husbands beat them

      They'd

Rather be brutes slumbering
Under it all

                 but still—the boy

What could he possibly be doing
                 out on a night like this

                 bare feet lifeless asphalt

             a man's sullied V-neck for a makeshift nightshirt

                              pulls the phone from its receiver
                              trembling from fear and frost of night
                              struggles to deposit coin in slot

He lingered for so long

                    he couldn't speak

              what is the nature of your emergency

Murmured it at last

                    Hello. Hello. Hell—

ERASURE

it starts with

        scoffs

      the knocking over of things

hollow tree trunk ocelot skin

        yaohuehuetl

a man speaking over a PA

    singing

    music playing

an inaudible laugh

          gunshots firing

rubber bullets

          water canons

a sign that reads

      stop the removals

   a lighter clicks

     breath of benzene

somewhere in the distance

babies crying women screaming thunder rumbling dogs barking
whistle blowing sobbing sirens screeching footsteps approaching

and still the drums

beyond the barricades

the indistinct whispers

of white men

sound just like a restless rivulet

can something be 62 percent water and 38 percent arsenic

INCIPIENT

someone   that loves

                         the ignition of small fires

            left

to save   himself   I mean

ceiling height   and thermal layering

caused the flashover

nothing spontaneous
about this kind of combustion

            I too

            burned

seven breaths until my throat seared

and yet again

we keep this   between us

and again

you go

I turn my back

close my eyes

count to ten

now fully developed

I inherit   the slag

but I will not accept   so he says

again

decay is not the most dangerous stage of fire

I softly kiss my father's cheek

whisper in his ear

I know father

but it is the longest

SOUTH ON I-45 DALLAS TO HUNTSVILLE

Can you tell me about the prison?

Nothing

I cannot tell you
how many armed guards
are stationed in the tower,
only

blood formed from this

offense

nor can I recall
color of mortar,
maze that was
path to visitation

only your voice

los corridos
cab of Dodge
filled with song.

In the end where will I dwell?

Nothing

ends mi'jo.

We are

breath

without check.

VIEW FROM THE FIFTH FLOOR OF THE ADAM HATS BUILDING, 1986

Mi'jo   you see that

                                                    dark façade,

Magnolia Hotel
                         odd mythic creature

gentrified   pegasus,   hips

of flesh—or   semblance of flesh—   tor-
so of brick and glass,

                                                    obsidian-
clad shoulders

                                                    dominating

diminishing

                         a reflection,

far bigger than mannequin,

opposite.

Glass, stone, steel

what they call progress

we call theft.

They will come mi'jo

blue suits

yellow dragons

they will come and take all of this

from us.

OF MUSKETS AND MAÍZ

when he

discovered her

my father   gave my mother
some of that   christopher columbus type love
conquered her   because she was beautiful
stripped her   of everything

and left her   bare

but even after all this   she still longed
for his kiss   dug her fingers

into his flesh   like

he was the shore   after a long journey at sea
this is where I come from   this is me

I am a child

of

muskets

and

maíz

ACKNOWLEDGEMENTS

Grateful acknowledgement is given to the editors of the following journals and anthologies in which earlier versions of these poems appeared:

Green Mountains Review: "Full Moon Pantoum" and "Of Muskets and Maíz"
Di-Verse-City: "The Lengths"
¡Manteca! An Anthology of Afro-Latin@ Poets: "Archetypes"
Southwestern American Literature: "Iris" and "The Corner of Bonita Blvd and Henderson Ave"
Huizache: "Mestizo" and "Nahui Ehecatl Second Son Wind Sun"
Sonora Review: "Nahui Ocelotl First Son Jaguar Sun"

Thank you to the Institute of American Indian Arts, every mentor/professor there who helped me along the way through my MFA and this manuscript including Joan Naviyuk Kane, Sherwin Bitsui, James Aronhióta's Stevens, Natalie Diaz, Jon Davis, Rachel Eliza Griffiths, and especially Santee Frazier. To the Lannan Foundation who generously helped fund part of my MFA, thank you. Thank you to my MFA cohort for their insights and feedback on many of these poems and for their friendship. To Michaelsun Stonesweat Knapp, you must know many of these poems are stronger because of you. So am I. Thank you to my sounding boards for these poems, Natasha Carrizosa and Elizabeth Powell. Much gratitude to The Frost Place Conference on Poetry and to Blas Falconer and Elizabeth Powell for believing in my work. To Kristine and Jay Snodgrass and the entire team at Anhinga Press thank you so damn much for all of this. To Eduardo C. Corral, you are a force for truth and Light. I will be eternally grateful to you for making *Arsonist* possible. Unbounded gratefulness to Layli Long Soldier, Eduardo C. Corral, and Juan Felipe Herrera for offering to read the manuscript and offer their thoughts on these poems. To Juan Felipe, maestro, you are right, there are more poems and stories behind the table serving coffee and lemonade at the fundraiser than in front of it. I hope these poems honor my family and friends (especially Tom and Fran Blueher and Jeff and Diane Davis) who have helped me in so many ways during the creation of *Arsonist*. To my Abuelo, thank you for placing the book in my hands. Tenías razón sobre las palabras, son un santuario. To my mother and brothers, thank you. Finding you my long, lost brother Mauricio and your beautiful daughters while writing these poems after all these years apart has filled my life with so much joy and Light.

To my daughters, Aiyana and Dakota, thank you for being you and inspiring me every day to write and live more deeply. To my beautiful partner Aída, we have walked this Path hand in hand. None of this would have been possible without you. Thank you.

And lastly to my father, it has taken me all these years to learn that just because you turned your back on me does not mean I have to do the same to you. This book is everything I would have said to you if given the chance.

I was able to speak to my silent mother not so long ago and tell her what I wanted to tell you both for so long. So I'm speaking to you now father, not in death, but at the age you were when you left me all those years ago. Half the age I am now.

Father. I am grateful for every second of my life. And I love you for being young and stupid and beautiful enough to let white arms embrace Brown skin. So I will not barter the beginning for a new place to end. I would simply say to you, thank you. Thank you for giving me life. Thank you for that one night when everything under the foolish moon told you, no. You said, yes. And that has made all the difference.

About the Author

Joaquín Zihuatanejo received his MFA in creative writing with a concentration in poetry from the Institute of American Indian Arts in Santa Fe, New Mexico. His work has been published in *Prairie Schooner, Yellow Medicine Review, Sonora Review, Southwestern American Literature,* and *Huizache* among other journals and anthologies. His poetry has been featured on HBO, NBC, and on NPR in Historias and The National Teacher's Initiative. Joaquín has two passions in his life, his wife Aída and poetry, always in that order.

ANHINGA PRESS